Experiments With Magnets

DALE-MARIE BRYAN

Children's Press®
An Imprint of Scholastic Inc.
New York   Toronto   London   Auckland   Sydney
Mexico City   New Delhi   Hong Kong
Danbury, Connecticut

Content Consultant
Suzanne E. Willis, PhD
Professor and Assistant Chair, Department of Physics
Northern Illinois University
DeKalb, Illinois

Library of Congress Cataloging-in-Publication Data

Bryan, Dale-Marie, 1953–
 Experiments with magnets/Dale Marie Bryan.
   p. cm.—(A true book)
 Includes bibliographical references and index.
 ISBN-13: 978-0-531-26345-7 (lib. bdg.)   ISBN-13: 978-0-531-26645-8 (pbk.)
 ISBN-10: 0-531-26345-2 (lib. bdg.)   ISBN-10: 0-531-26645-1 (pbk.)
 1. Magnetism—Experiments—Juvenile literature. 2. Magnets—Juvenile
literature. I. Title. II. Series.
 QC755.3.B79 2012
 538'.4078—dc22   2011009492

All rights reserved. Published in 2012 by Children's Press, an imprint of Scholastic Inc.
Printed in China 62
SCHOLASTIC, CHILDREN'S PRESS, A TRUE BOOK, and associated logos are trademarks and/or registered trademarks of Scholastic Inc.

1 2 3 4 5 6 7 8 9 10 R 21 20 19 18 17 16 15 14 13 12

Find the Truth!

Everything you are about to read is true *except* for one of the sentences on this page.

Which one is **TRUE**?

T or F Compass needles are attracted to the geographic North Pole.

T or F Earth's magnetic force is caused by its molten iron core.

Find the answers in this book.

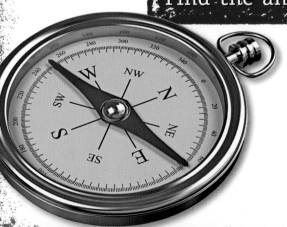

3

Contents

THE **BIG** TRUTH!

Our Mega Magnet

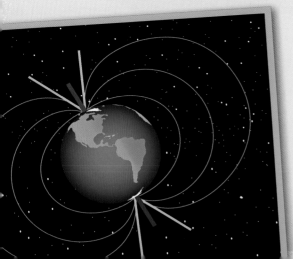

An illustration of Earth's magnetic fields

Experimenting with cereal and a magnet

Many roller coasters
use magnets to
move their cars.

A scientist in the 16th century studies a lodestone, which is magnetic.

CHAPTER 1

Scientists' Questions

Long ago, ancient people **observed** that certain stones attracted iron. They thought it was magic. Some may have wondered how the stones worked. Today, we know that such stones are magnetic. Scientists study magnetism by doing experiments and making observations of their own. When they do this, they use the scientific method. It is a step-by-step way to find answers.

Early scientists were often called philosophers.

The microscope was invented in 1590.

How It Works

This is how the scientific method works. First, a scientist pulls together all the observations about something. Next, he or she thinks up a question that the observations don't explain. Then the scientist forms a **hypothesis**. This is what the scientist believes is the correct answer to the question. It must be a statement that can be tested. Next, he or she plans out an experiment to test it.

During the experiment, the scientist writes down everything that happens. Finally, the scientist looks at how the experiment turned out and draws a **conclusion**.

Sometimes, the conclusion is that the hypothesis is correct. Other times, it turns out that the hypothesis was not correct. Then it's time to come up with a new hypothesis and design another experiment.

Scientists sometimes have to rethink their original hypotheses.

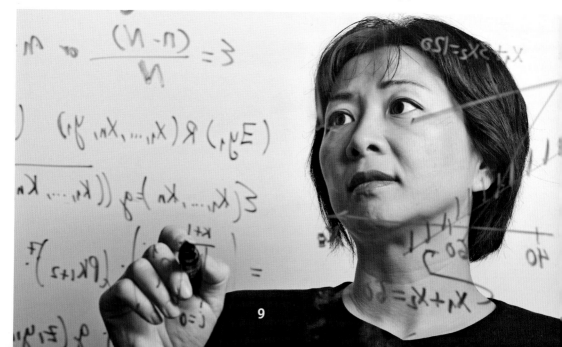

Careful Work

Scientists must be very careful when they run experiments. They must measure everything. They carefully record each step of the experiment. They write down measurements and other observations in notebooks or on computers. If they ever need to repeat an experiment, they can look at their notes. They can use them to do the same experiment again the exact same way.

Some tools are specially designed to make very small, or very large, measurements.

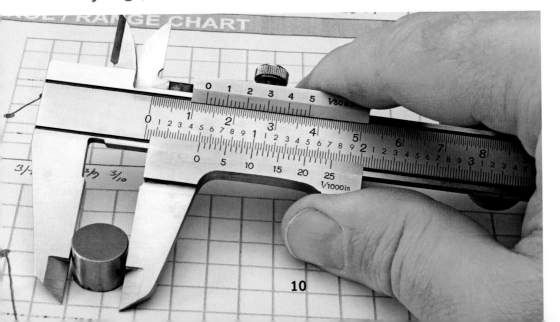

Many major discoveries have been made by accident!

Scientists often use graphs to help understand the results of an experiment.

Scientists must also be open-minded. Sometimes experiments do not turn out as expected. An incorrect hypothesis can be disappointing, but scientists need to be willing to learn from such experiences.

Magnets can hold paper, pictures, or other decorations on a refrigerator.

CHAPTER 2

Magnets in the Making

To understand magnets, we must first look at **elements** and **atoms**. All matter is composed of elements or combinations of elements. An element is a material made up of just one kind of atom. Atoms are extremely tiny pieces of matter. Gold is an element composed only of gold atoms. Water is a combination of two elements—oxygen and hydrogen. Steel is a combination of iron, carbon, and other elements.

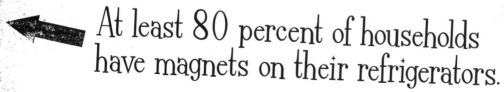

At least 80 percent of households have magnets on their refrigerators.

What Is an Atom?

Atoms are the small particles that make up elements. Inside each atom is a **nucleus** containing one or more **protons**. Spinning madly about the nucleus are one or more **electrons**. Protons and electrons are electrically charged. Each proton has a positive charge, and each electron has a negative one. Usually, atoms have the same number of protons and electrons. Their positive and negative charges balance each other out.

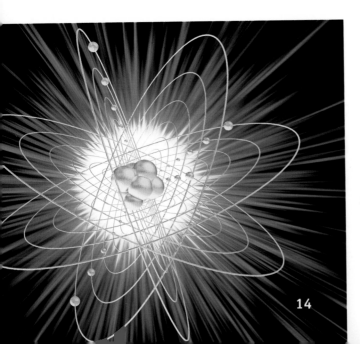

Each element's atoms have a specific number of protons.

Extremely high heat can cause a magnet to lose its magnetism.

Magnets attract paper clips and other items containing certain metals.

Where Do Magnets Fit In?

Magnets come in all shapes and sizes. But it's their spinning electrons that make them work. When electrons spin, they create the tiniest of magnetic fields. In certain metals, such as iron and nickel, the tiny magnetic fields of the atoms influence other atoms and cause them to line up. All of these little aligned magnetic fields add up to create a bigger field. The metal is then a magnet.

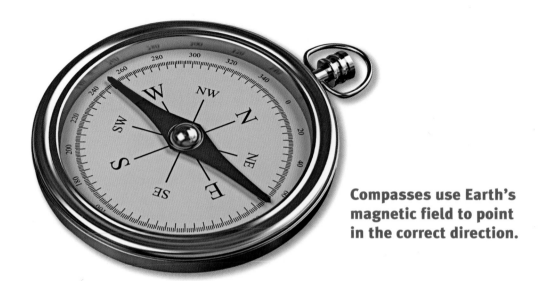

Compasses use Earth's magnetic field to point in the correct direction.

Magnetic Poles

The spinning electrons of all elements create little magnetic fields. But the fields don't line up to create a magnetic field in all elements. It only does that in certain metallic elements.

When a magnetic bar hangs from a thread and is held level, one end always points toward Earth's north magnetic pole. We call that end of the bar its north pole. The opposite end is called its south pole.

Nature-Made Magnets

Lodestones are natural magnets. They are made of a substance called **magnetite**. Magnetite contains iron, but not all magnetite is magnetic. Some scientists believe that lodestones formed when lightning struck magnetite. They think that the electricity caused its atoms to line up in the same direction. In an experiment, scientists placed magnetite crystals in an area where lightning strikes frequently. Over time, the crystals became magnetized lodestones.

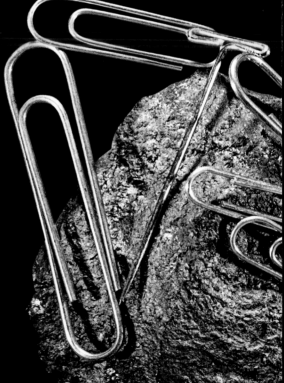

Our Mega Magnet

Earth itself is one big magnet. Its core is solid iron surrounded by churning **molten** iron. The churning iron creates a huge magnetic field with two poles. The north magnetic pole is in northern Canada. The south magnetic pole is in the Antarctic region. These are different from Earth's geographic poles. Globes show the north and south geographic poles. They are the points around which Earth rotates.

Earth's solid iron core is about the same size as the moon.

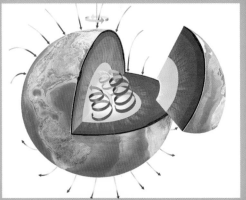

Earth's magnetic field extends out into space.

Particles from the sun move through Earth's magnetic field and produce these unusual lights. The lights appear mainly at Earth's poles.

Playing With Your Food

Now let's look at how magnets work. We'll do a demonstration first.

Demonstration: What's Magnetic?

Materials:

- ▶ **strong bar magnet (you can find these at hardware or home improvement stores)**
- ▶ **7 or 8 different metal objects, such as paper clips, coins, keys, or thumbtacks**

Which items around the house are attracted to magnets?

Procedure:

Pass the magnet over the objects.

Observe: **Does the magnet cause the objects to move?**

What happened? **The objects that contain iron will jump onto the magnet. Steel objects usually jump toward the magnet as well, because steel contains iron. Anything made of pure nickel should also move toward the magnet. However, nickel coins actually contain only a small amount of nickel, so they do nothing as the magnet passes over them. Now let's do some experiments to find where iron exists in other items.**

Cereal often contains iron and other metals.

Experiment #1: Breakfast of Champions

Observe: Many cereals are advertised as containing iron.

Research question: Does cereal contain the kind of iron that is attracted to magnets?

True Book hypothesis: Some cereals contain iron, which attracts them to magnets.

Materials:
- **cereal bowl**
- **water**
- **strong magnet**
- **1 serving of Total® brand cereal**

Gather these materials together.

Procedure:

1. Fill the bowl with water.

2. Crush the cereal flakes into very small pieces with your hands. Don't crush them so much that they turn into powder.

3. Gently sprinkle the cereal pieces onto the water's surface.

4. Hold the magnet about 0.25 inch (0.6 centimeter) above some floating cereal pieces. Be careful not to breathe on the bowl!

5. Slowly move the magnet to the left or right.

Step 4

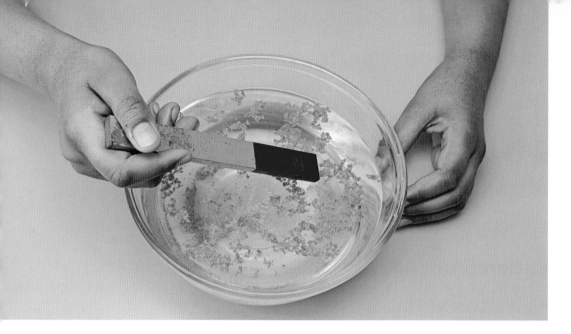

Did the cereal follow the magnet?

Record your results: Do the cereal pieces follow the magnet?

Conclusion: Total® contains enough iron that the pieces are attracted to the magnet. The attraction was not strong enough to make the pieces jump to the magnet. However, the attraction was strong enough for the pieces to follow the magnet around the bowl. Does this match your observations? Was the True Book hypothesis correct?

Magnetic Pots

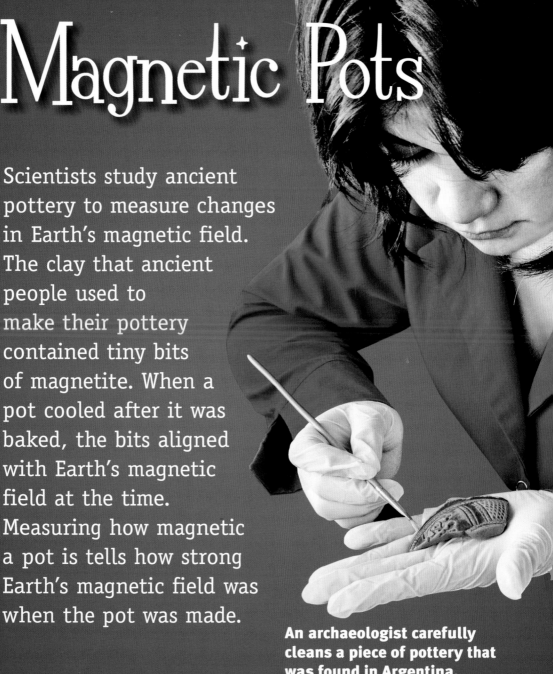

Scientists study ancient pottery to measure changes in Earth's magnetic field. The clay that ancient people used to make their pottery contained tiny bits of magnetite. When a pot cooled after it was baked, the bits aligned with Earth's magnetic field at the time. Measuring how magnetic a pot is tells how strong Earth's magnetic field was when the pot was made.

An archaeologist carefully cleans a piece of pottery that was found in Argentina.

Experiment #2: How Much Iron?

Research question: Do other cereals contain enough iron to follow the magnet?

True Book hypothesis: Other cereals containing iron can be moved around the bowl by the magnet.

Materials:
- ▶ **the cereal bowl, water, and magnet used in the previous experiment (p. 22)**
- ▶ **1 serving each of other kinds of cereal containing high levels of iron**

What other cereals contain enough iron to follow a magnet?

26

Procedure: Repeat the procedure used in the previous experiment (p. 23), this time using another kind of cereal. You can repeat the experiment for each kind of cereal you have collected.

Record your results: Do the cereal pieces follow the magnet?

Conclusion: Many cereals contain iron, but not as pure iron. The magnet does not move cereals that do not contain pure iron. Does this match your observations? Was the True Book hypothesis correct?

Nutrition Facts

Serving Size 1/4 Cup (30g)
Servings Per Container About 38

Amount Per Serving

Calories 200 Calories from Fat 150

	% Daily Value*
Total Fat 17g	**26%**
Saturated Fat 2.5g	**13%**
Trans Fat 0g	
Cholesterol 0mg	**0%**
Sodium 120mg	**5%**
Total Carbohydrate 7g	**2%**
Dietary Fiber 2g	**8%**
Sugars 1g	
Protein 5g	

Vitamin A 0%	•	Vitamin C 0%
Calcium 4%	•	Iron 8%

*Percent Daily Values are based on a 2,000 calorie diet.

What happened? Iron is sometimes combined with other elements in cereal. When iron atoms combine with atoms of other elements, their magnetism can become very weak or disappear altogether.

People need iron to stay healthy.

CHAPTER 4

Magnets at Work

Early sailors found that lodestones lined up in the direction of the North Star. This helped them find their way on the seas. Today, we use instruments called **compasses** to find magnetic north. A compass contains a magnet that floats on a pin or in liquid. The Chinese made the first compasses about 2,000 years ago. We will use a modern-day compass in our experiments.

Early Chinese compasses were made of lodestones and bronze plates.

Demonstration: Misdirection

First, we'll demonstrate how a compass works.

Materials:

► **lensatic compass, which has a small lens for navigation and a floating platform (from a discount or sporting goods store)**

► **round button magnet**

Gather these two items.

Procedure:

1. Open the compass and set it on a flat surface.

2. Let its floating platform come to rest, with its arrow pointing to magnetic north.

3. Bring the flat side of the magnet toward the compass's West mark. What happens?

4. Flip the magnet to bring its opposite side toward the compass. What happens now?

Observe: How did the compass react to the different sides of the magnet?

What happened? One side of the magnet should cause the compass arrow to swing away from it. The magnet's opposite side should cause the arrow to swing toward it. This shows how opposite magnetic poles attract each other. The compass needle's north pole swung toward the magnet's south pole. It was **repelled** by the magnet's north pole.

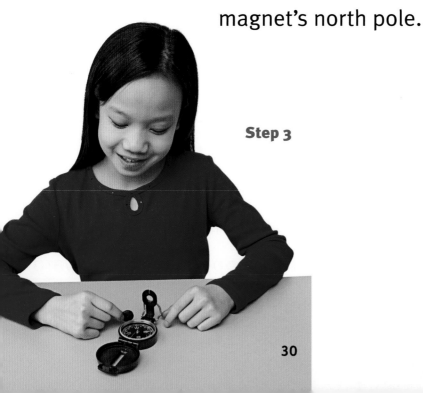

Step 3

30

Experiment #1: Big or Small?

Observe: Magnets affect a compass.

Research question: Would adding more magnets make a difference?

True Book hypothesis: More magnets will have a stronger effect on a compass.

Materials:
- lensatic compass
- 3 bar magnets, all the same size
- helper
- pencil
- masking tape

You will need a helper for this experiment.

Procedure:

1. Place a piece of masking tape about 30 inches (76 cm) long on a flat surface.

2. Set the compass at one end of the taped line and let its floating platform come to rest.

3. Let all three magnets clamp together. Place them at the other end of the taped line.

4. Slide the magnets slowly toward the compass. Keep your fingers and other objects out of the magnet's path.

5. Have your helper watch the compass and announce when the platform begins to swing.

Step 4

6. Stop moving the magnets. Mark their position.

7. Pull off one of the magnets from the stack.

8. Place the stack of two magnets on the end of the taped line.

9. Slide the magnets toward the compass until your helper says to stop.

10. Mark the magnet's position.

Record your results: Which mark is farther from the compass?

Conclusion: The larger stack of magnets should move the compass from a greater distance. When magnets are combined, their strength also combines. Does this match your observations? Was the True Book hypothesis correct?

Step 10

Experiment #2: Make a Magnet

Step 3

Observe: Paper clips are attracted to magnets.

Research question: Can a paper clip also be used as a magnet?

True Book hypothesis: A paper clip can turn into a magnet.

Materials:
- **lensatic compass**
- **large paper clip**
- **bar magnet**

Procedure:

1. Place the compass on a flat surface.
2. Hold the paper clip next to the compass's East or West point. Does the platform move?
3. Place the paper clip on the magnet for about 10 seconds.
4. Hold it next to the compass's East or West point.

Record your results: Does the compass platform move the first time? Does it move after the paper clip has been held to the magnet?

Conclusion: The paper clip should move the compass platform after being held to the magnet. The magnet temporarily turned the paper clip into a magnet. While it was held to the magnet, its atoms became magnetically aligned to the nearest pole of the magnet. This gave the paper clip a magnetic field of its own. Does this match your observations? Was the True Book hypothesis correct?

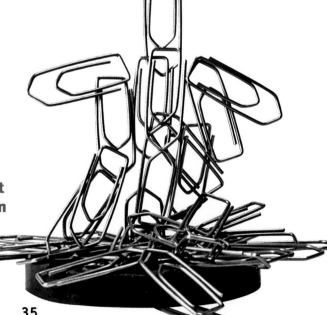

A paper clip touching a magnet becomes a magnet itself. It can attract other paper clips.

CHAPTER 5

Electromagnets

In the 1820s, Hans Oersted discovered that he could create magnets by using electrical currents. These are called electromagnets. Electromagnets work when electricity passing through a wire coil sets up a magnetic field. Electromagnets can push or pull, depending on the direction and force of the electrical current.

Let's make an electromagnet as a demonstration.

Roller coasters use electromagnets to push the cars along the track.

Demonstration: Building an Electromagnet

Be Safe: You should have an adult help you when you experiment with electricity.

Materials:

- iron rod 5 inches (13 cm) long, such as a nail or piece of rebar
- about 6 feet (1.8 meter) of magnet wire (from an electronics store or hobby shop)
- 1 D battery
- electrical tape
- pile of paper clips
- fine sandpaper

Procedure:

1. Dab the iron rod in the paper clips. Is it magnetic?

2. Use sandpaper to rub the coating off both ends of the wire.

3. Wrap the wire snugly around the rod. Leave about 6 inches (15 cm) at each end.

4. Tape one end of the wire to the negative (flat) end of the battery.

5. Tape the other end of the wire to the positive end of the battery.

6. Dab the rod onto the paper clip pile again.

Observe: The rod is now magnetic.

What happened? An electric current runs from the positive end of the battery, through the wire, to the battery's negative end. The wire carries this current through the rod, making the rod magnetic.

Step 3

Be Safe: Remove one end of the wire from the battery after every experiment. Leaving both ends can cause things to get hot.

Experiment #1: What's in a Spoon?

Observe: Silverware looks like it contains metal that could be magnetic.

Research question: Can a spoon be used to make an electromagnet?

True Book hypothesis: A metal spoon can be used in an electromagnet.

Be Safe: You should have an adult help you when you experiment with electricity.

Materials:

- a spoon
- paper clips
- fine sandpaper
- magnet wire
- 1 D battery
- electrical tape

Procedure: Follow the steps used in the demonstration (p. 37), this time using a spoon instead of an iron rod.

Record your results: Was the spoon able to pick up the paper clips?

Conclusion: Silverware is often made out of stainless steel, which is usually not magnetic. Even silverware made out of pure silver is not very magnetic. This means your electromagnet probably did not work. Does this match your observations? Was the True Book hypothesis correct?

Experiment #2: Is Bigger Better?

Research question: Would a bigger battery make a more powerful electromagnet?

True Book hypothesis: A D battery does not make a stronger electromagnet than a AA battery does.

Be Safe: You should have an adult help you when you experiment with electricity.

Materials:

- 1 AA battery
- iron rod
- paper clips
- fine sandpaper
- magnet wire
- 1 D battery
- electrical tape

Timeline of Magnets

1100s
Lodestones are used for navigation.

1269
Petrus de Maricourt finds that magnets have two poles.

Procedure:

1. Make an electromagnet like the one used in the demonstration (p. 37).
2. Dab the rod into the pile of paper clips. How many can it pick up?
3. Remove the D battery from the electromagnet.
4. Hook the wire ends to the positive and negative ends of the AA battery.
5. Dab the rod into the pile of paper clips.

Record your results: Which time was the rod able to pick up the most paper clips?

1600
William Gilbert discovers Earth's magnetism and magnetic poles.

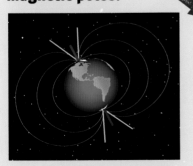

1820
Hans Christian Oersted discovers that a wire carrying a current creates a magnetic field.

Conclusion: Both electromagnets should pick up around the same number of paper clips. Both the D battery and the AA battery produce the same size current. Does this match your observations? Was the True Book hypothesis correct?

We know magnets aren't magical as ancient people believed. If you have questions about magnets, you can use the scientific method to discover much more about how magnets work. ★

What other experiments can you create using magnets?

Cost to use one of the big magnets at the Mag Lab: $4,000 per hour

How much weaker Earth's magnetic field is than a typical bar magnet: 1,000 times

How hot you have to get an iron magnet to take away its magnetic properties: 1,500 °F (800 °C)

The weight of the world's largest suspended electromagnet: 88 tons

Unit used to measure magnetic strength: Tesla, named for Nikola Tesla

The number of permanent magnets in your home or car: 50

Did you find the truth?

F Compass needles are attracted to the geographic North Pole.

T Earth's magnetic force is caused by its molten iron core.

Resources

Books

Flaherty, Michael. *Electricity & Batteries*. New York: PowerKids Press, 2008.

Flaherty, Michael. *Magnetism & Magnets*. Brookfield, CT: Copper Beech Books, 1999.

Galus, Pamela J. *Science Fair Projects: An Inquiry-Based Guide Grades 5–8*. Greensboro, NC: Carson-Dellosa Publishing Co., 2003.

Murray, Julie. *Magnets*. Edina, MN: ABDO, 2007.

Taylor-Butler, Christine. *Junior Scientists: Experiment With Magnets*. Ann Arbor, MI: Cherry Lake Publishing, 2010.

Walker, Sally M. *Magnetism*. Minneapolis: Lerner Publications, 2006.

Organizations and Web Sites

Magnet Man: Cool Experiments With Magnets

www.coolmagnetman.com/magindex.htm

Find information, and a wide variety of experiments and links about magnets and electricity.

Physics4Kids — Electricity and Magnetism

www.physics4kids.com/files/elec_intro.html

Discover information about magnets and electricity along with quizzes to test what you've learned.

Places to Visit

expERIEnce Children's Museum

420 French Street
Erie, PA 16507
(814) 453-3743
www.eriechildrensmuseum.org

See the *Explore the History, Mystery, and Magic of Magnets* exhibit, and learn about magnets at six interactive stations.

Temecula Children's Museum

42081 Main Street
Temecula, CA 92590
(951) 308-6376
www.pennypickles.org

Take part in some hands-on activities with magnets in Professor Pennypickle's Workshop.

Important Words

atoms (AT-uhmz)—the tiniest parts of elements that have all the properties of that element

compasses (KOM-puhss-uz)—devices for determining direction

conclusion (kuhn-KLOO-zhun)— a final decision

electrons (i-LEK-trahnz)—tiny, negatively charged particles that move around the nucleus of an atom

elements (EL-uh-muhntz)—substances that cannot be divided up into simpler substances

hypothesis (hy-PAH-thuh-siss)—a prediction that can be tested about how a scientific experiment or investigation will turn out

lodestones (LODE-stonz)—rare pieces of magnetite that can attract iron

magnetite (MAG-nuh-tyt)—a type of rock that contains iron and can become magnetized

molten (MOLE-tuhn)—melted

nucleus (NOO-klee-uhs)—the central part of an atom that is made up of neutrons and protons

observed (ub-ZERVD)—watched

protons (PROH-tahnz)—positively charged particles inside a nucleus

repelled (rih-PELD)—pushed away

Index

Page numbers in **bold** indicate illustrations

About the Author

Dale-Marie Bryan has an elementary education degree and taught school for 14 years. This is her fifth book for children. She has also published stories, articles, and poems in magazines such as *Highlights* and *Wee Wisdom*. Dale-Marie has always been "attracted" to magnets, and has two pet lodestones she calls Iron Man and Magneto.

PHOTOGRAPHS © 2012: Alamy Images: 40 right (INTERFOTO), 5 bottom, 36 (LHB Photo), 10 (Lyroky), 25 (Picture Contact BV); iStockphoto: 19 bottom, 43 bottom (Roman Krochuk), 3, 16 (onurdongel), 9 (Francisco Romero); Ken Karp: back cover, 5 top, 20, 22, 23, 24, 26, 29, 30, 31, 32, 33, 34, 37, 38, 39, 42; Media Bakery: 14 (Science Photo Library), 12 (Somos Images), 11; Photo Researchers, NY: 17 (Joel Arem), 19 top (Gary Hincks), 28, 40 left (Science Source); Scholastic Library Publishing, Inc.: 44; Science Photo Library/Sheila Terry: 41 right; ShutterStock, Inc.: 18 background, 19 background (CnApTaK), cover, 15 (luchschen), 21 (Monkey Business Images), 8 (Radu Razvan), 35 (SergeyIT), 4, 19 center, 41 left (Snowbelle), 27 (XAOC); Superstock, Inc./Science and Society: 6.